Through the Deductive Method
Pastoral Theology

Through the Deductive Method Pastoral Theology

© Kwang Young Bae, 2016

1판 1쇄 인쇄 __ 2016년 03월 20일
1판 1쇄 발행 __ 2016년 03월 30일

지은이 __ 배광영
펴낸이 __ 이종엽

펴낸곳 __ 글모아 출판
　　　　등록 __ 제324-2005-42호

공급처 __ (주)글로벌콘텐츠출판그룹
　　　　대표 __ 홍정표　이사 __ 양정섭　디자인 __ 김미미　편집 __ 송은주　기획·마케팅 __ 노경민　경영지원 __ 안선영
　　　　주소 __ 서울특별시 강동구 천중로 196 정일빌딩 401호　전화 __ 02-488-3280　팩스 __ 02-488-3281
　　　　홈페이지 __ www.gcbook.co.kr

값 12,000원
ISBN 978-89-94626-41-3 03230

Through the Deductive Method
Pastoral Theology

By Kwang Young Bea

Professor

Calvin theological Seminary

글모아출판

Preface

Praise the Lord, Praise the Lord, oh my soul.

I will praise the Lord all my life.

I will sing praise to my God as long as I live.

Psalm 146:1-2

It become my one's view of life on the word of Psalm.

He who gives to me is powerful and almighty God.

I give thanks to God with my whole heart.

Because I think that God gives me ability to write this book.

I only hope that I help them to read this book.

I also only praise God.

CONTENTS

Through the Deductive Method
Pastoral Theology

About Pastoral theology

1. What is the connection point of Pastoral theology?

Pastoral theology is medical center for the Christianity.

Who is the master of medical center of Christianity?

It is only God.

Look at the Bible.

Mt16:18 - I tell you that you are Peter and on this rock I will build my church and the gates of Hades will not overcome it.

Ex25:8,9 - Then have them make a sanctuary for me and I will dwell among them Make this tabernacle and all its furnishings exactly like the pattern I will show you.

Ps132:13 - For the Lord has chosen Zion has desired it for his dwelling.

Who are the church?

They are the people whom God called according to God's will.

Jn6:65 - He went on to say this is Why I told that no one can come to me unless the Father has enabled him

Eph1:5 - He predestined us to be adopted as his sons through

Jesus Christ in accordance with his pleasure and will.

2Ti 1:9 - Who has saved us and called us to a holy life not because of anything we have done but because of his own purpose and grace, this grace was given us in Christ Jesus before the beginning of time.

1 Co 3:16 - Don't you know that you yourselves are God's temple and God's Spirit lives in you?

1. Pastoral theology should be known that Pastors themselves should be using Biblical theology, dogmatics theology and practical theology.

1. Pastoral theology should be called the Holy Spirit's theology which is if Holy Spirit goes anywhere, we also have to go, if Holy Spirit doesn't go anywhere, we mustn't go there.

1. We have to know that God is himself.

Martin Buber said: "All in the world divided into three forms that become one."

"I" in the grammatically is the first person.

"You" in the grammatically is the second person.

"It, they, he and she" in the grammatically are the third person.

Who are you from "me-which is yourself"?

God is only you for "me-which is yourself".

If so there are husband, wife, parent and children, as the third persons.

I think one more.

I myself am also in the third persons from me, because I don't know perfectly my thinking, but God knows my mind and account of our hair.

Let us look at

Mt 10:30 - And even the very hair of your head are all numbered.

Jn 1:48 - Hoe do you know me? Nathanael asked, Jesus answered I saw you while you were still under the fig tree before Philip called you.

Ps 139: 2 - You know when I sit and when I rise you perceive my thoughts from afar.

So God is only you for me. (which is yourself.)

1. Pastoral Theology should has been admitted the sovereign power of God.

God goes day and day and with each passing moment with me.

The Calvin said to us

If the Bible says to the human, we also can say, if the Bible doesn't say, we can't say anything.

We haven't got our time, our way and our power but we only have God's time, God's way and God's power.

Ps 119 : 105 - The word of the Lord is the light of our way and the lamp of our step.

Jer 32 : 17 - Ah Sovereign Lord you have made the heaven and the earth by your great power and outstretched arm, Nothing is too harsh for you.

1. Pastoral Theology doesn't say about destined but God's will be.

Gal 2:20 - I have been crucified with Christ I no longer live but Christ lives in me The life I live in the body I live by faith in the name of the Son of the God who loves me and gave Himself for me.

As Paul said

If I myself died, God lives in me.

So Christianity isn't being destined. We only have to go following according to Holy Spirit.

1. The cosmos is the one with the time and space, matter and antimatter.

The cosmos has been made as united because it starts as united. If the cosmos is a summary as simple, the cosmos is the one and we can speak that it is the human. If the cosmos is to reduce, it become a small ball.

The cosmos is the one which the expanse was made from the dust of identity as an expanse. The Bible said that the dust of identity is called the dust of the ground.

Ge 2:7 - The lord God formed the man from the dust of the ground and breathed into His nostrils the breath of life, and the man became a living being.

The Bible also can reduce as one sentence (synopsis) which is about Christ Jesus.

When we know that the cosmos is to become the one, we can speak with relation of one another.

Jn 17: 21 - That all of them may be one, Father, just as you are in me and I am in You. May they also be in us so that the world may believe that you have sent me.

Act 26:26 - From one man he made every nation of men, that they should inhabit the whole earth .

Gal 3:28 - There is neither Jew nor Greek, slave nor free, male nor female, for you are all one in Christ Jesus.

Yes, it is true that the God and the human and the cosmos are one in Christ Jesus.

1. It is a point of meeting with God and Christianity is at death as God's died and Christianity's died.

It is really the core of all of them.

While Christ Jesus lives in the world, how did He lives?

He died on the cross for us.

By His death, he was obeying of the Law of God.

So if we also obey the Law of God, we have to be died like Christ Jesus.

His death was the completion of the Law of God.

When we also died like Christ Jesus, we can complete to the Law of God.

His death was the model of our live.

So we have to die like Christ Jesus.

1. The Christianity can live whenever and wherever is happy and health.

Ge 13:9 - Is not the whole land before you? Let's part company. If you go to the left, I'll go the right; if you go to the right, I'll go to the left.

Ph 3:16 - Only let us up and to what we have already attained.

Ps 23:1

The Lord is my shepherd , I shall not be in want.

Ph 4:13 - I can do everything through Him who gives me strength.

Excise

1. What do you think about Pastoral theology?

2. Who are the church?

3. What do pastors know about that?

4. Who are only you from me?

5. What does pastoral theology admit?

6. Is the christianity only destined?

7. How many kind has cosmos made?

8. What is the point of meeting God and Christianity?

9. What is meaning on the crossing Christ Jesus?

About Pastoral Theology is always present

1. God's time is always present namely is doing. but the human lives with past, present and future.

Rev 22: 13 - I am the Alpha and the Omega, the First and the Last, the Beginning and the Last.

Psa 90:1,2 - Lord, You have been our dwelling place throughout all generations. Before the mountain were born or you brought forth the earth and the world, from everlasting to everlasting you are God.

Mt 28:20 - God is with you and always to the very end of the age.

If so, we also have to live as present always.

1. The Christianity can always laugh as we are looking at ourselves.

Phi 4:12-13 - I know what it is to be in need, and I know what it is to have plenty. I have learned the secret of being content in any and every situation, whether well fed or hungry, whether living in plenty or in want.

I can do everything through Him who gives me strength.

1Th 5 16-18 - Be joyful always, pray continually, give thanks in all circumstance this is God will for you in Christ Jesus.

Why can't we laugh? Because we left God.

1. We always meet an event while we live in the world.

The event is all of things from living breath or stopping breath.

For example,

The events are born, death, meeting, leaving, giving, taking, gain, loss, love, hate etc at all of the universe.

When we use the events unless we live our gain for life if we live for the glory of God, we always can live as happy and health.

So we live for the glory of God.

Dt 8:3 - He humbled you, causing you to hunger and then feeding you with manna, which neither you nor your fathers had known, to teach you that man does not live on bread alone but on every word that comes from the mouth of the Lord.

Ps 119:105 - Your word is a lamp to my feet and a light for my path.

Mt 6:34 - Therefore do not worry about tomorrow, for tomorrow will worry about itself, Each day has enough trouble of its own.

1Co 10: 31 - So whether you eat or drink or whatever you do, do it all for the glory of God.

1. The good tree bears good fruit and bad tree bears bad fruit.

This is a law of God which God made .

The good tree is living tree and living tree is always working for life. so it is always present.

1 Pe 5:4 - When the Chief Shepherd appears, you will receive the crown of glory that will never fade away.

Jn10:10 - The thief comes only to steal and kill and destroy; I have come that they may have life, have it to the full.

Ps 23:2 - He makes me lie down in green pastures, he leads me beside quiet waters.

By the way, the human becomes bad fruit to themselves. Because the human left God. If the human bears good fruit, they must come to God. If we come to God, we know that He is standing in our heart. My life is driven by Holy Spirit who comes in our heart.

1. We don't know that each of us comes when the last time.

So we are only on the present now.

Lk 12:20 - God said to him, You fool! This is very night your life will be demanded from you, Then who will get what you have prepared for yourself?

Ps 73:19 - How suddenly are they destroyed, completely swept away by terrors!

Ps 103: 15 - As for man, his days are like grass, he flourishes like a flower of the field.

Mt 6:34 - Therefore do not worry about tomorrow, for tomorrow will worry about itself. Each day has enough trouble of its own.

Exercise

1. When is Pastoral Theology always?

2. When until is God with Christianity?

3. How live the human dividing their life?

4. How could the Christianity always laugh?

5. What does the soul human eat to live?

6. What are that the good tree bears good fruit and bad tree bears bad fruit?

7. Why did the human come bad fruit?

About Pastoral

1. What is Pastoral?

Pastoral is only that God's will transmits to Christianity.

Dt 18:18 - I will raise up for them a prophet like you from among their brother; I will put my words in his mouth, and he will tell them everything I command him.

Jer 1:9 - Then the Lord reached out his hand and touched my mouth and said to me, Now, I have put my words in your mouth.

Ro 1:1 - Paul, a servant of Christ Jesus, called to be an apostle and set apart for the gospel of God.

Pastoral is job of pastor, the job of pastor is only on transmission.

1. Pastoral is that Christianity are looked like Christ Jesus as our model.

Jn 13:15 - I have set you an example that you should do as I have done for you

Eph 5:1 - Be imitators of God, therefore, as dearly loved children.

1Co 11:1 - Follow my example, as I follow the example of Christ.

Phi 3:17 - Join with others in following my example brothers and take note of those who live according to the pattern we gave you. The model of pastoral is only Christ Jesus.

1. Pastoral is that they are response to the word of God.

Nu 1:53 - The Levites are to be responsible for the care of the tabernacle of the Testimony.

Mt 5:13-14 - You are the salt of the earth. But if the salt loses its saltiness, how can it be made salty again? It is no longer good for anything, except to be thrown out and trampled by men. You are the light of the world. A city on a hill cannot be hidden.

1. Pastoral is that the Christianity become like God namely comes to be looked like Christ Jesus.

Jn 17:22 - I have given them the glory that you gave me, that they may be one as we are one;

Ga 3:28 - There is neither Jew nor Greek, slave nor free, make nor female, for you are all one in Christ Jesus.

Eph 2:22 - And in him you too are being built together to become a dwelling in which God lives by his Spirit.

EPh 4:15 - Instead, speaking the truth in love, we will in all things grow up into him who is the Head, that is, Christ.

God made human to make happy through doing like God and coming like Christ Jesus.

1. Pastoral is that Christianity takes to make a rest.

Ps 23:2 - He makes me lie down in green pastures, he leads me beside quiet waters.

Mt 11:28~30 - Come to me, all you who are weary and burdened, and I will give you rest. Take my yoke upon you and learn from me, for I am gentle and humble in heart, and you will find rest for your souls. For my yoke is easy and my burden si light.

Heb 4:10 - For anyone who enters God's rest also rests from his own work, just as God did from his.

1. Pastoral is that the Holy Spirit is the power.

Ac 1:8 - You will receive power when the Holy Spirit comes on you. you will be my witnesses in Jerusalem and in all Judea and Samaria and to the end on the earth.

Jn 14:26 - The counselor, the Holy Spirit whom the Father will send in my name, will teach you all things, and will remind you of everything I have said to you.

Jn 16:13~14 - When he, the Spirit of truth, comes, he will guide you into all truth. He will not speak on his own, He will speak only what He hears and He will tell you what is yet to come. He will bring to glory to me by taken from what is mine and making it known to you

Exercise

1. What is God's will transmits to Christianity?

2. What is purpose of pastoral?

3 What is purpose of Christianity?

4. Who is the model of Christianity?

5 Pastoral about what is response?

6. What does pastoral make for Christianity?

7. What is the power of Pastoral?

About the foundation of pastoral

1. The foundation of pastoral is the Bible.

Jn 1:1 - In the beginning was the word and the word was with God and the word was God.

Mt 5:17~18 - Do not think that I have come to abolish the Law or the Prophets; I have not come to abolish them but to fulfill them. I tell you the truth, until heaven and earth disappear, not the smallest letter, not the least stroke of a pen, will by any means disappear from the Law until everything is accomplished.

We have to live according to the Bible.

1. The Bible said to us that Jesus Christ came on the earth.

Jn 10:10 - I have come that they may have life and have it to the full.

Jn 21:15~17 - Simon Son of John, do you love Me? Jesus said Feed my sheep.

Ps 23:1 - The Lord is my Shepherd, I shall not be in want.

1. The Bible said to us about pastoral has got two circles.

Two circles came from the name of son of God.

When God came on the earth as human, His son's name has got two. One is Jesus Christ and the other is Immanuel.

The meaning of Jesus Christ is the savior and the meaning of Immanuel is that God is with us.

Mt 1:21, 23 - She will give birth to a son, and you are to give him the name Jesus, because he will save his people from their sins. The virgin will be with child and will give birth to a son, and they will call him Immanuel - which means, God with us.

It means that God is with us.

The meaning of God is with us, God has been died for us.

Exercise

1. What is the foundation of pastoral?

2. Where does say about Jesus Christ comes on the earth?

3. What do you find out the meaning through the name of the son of God?

4. what is the two circle?

5. What is the meaning of Jesus Christ?

6. What is the meaning of Immanuel?

1. What is historical foundation of Pastoral?

It is the theology.

The theology has got four circle.

They are

    *Biblical   theology

    *Dogmatics theology

    *Historical theology

    *Practical   theology

I have got another meaning.

I think that God gave the human identity through the doctrine.

It is about that there is to be and to do.

To be:

    *God

    *The human(Home)

    *The word of God(Bible)

    *The church(Nation)

    *The history(Nature)

To do:

   *The Law of Holy Father, Holy Son and Holy Spirit.

   *The Law of worship, faith and pray.

   *The Law of that the human is analysis and God is
   conclusion.

   *The Law of that there are only different explaining but
   really the meaning is the one.

   *The Law of reward is in accordance with a deeds.

   *The Law of that they all are say Yes.

Exercise

1. What is historical foundation of pastoral?

2. How much circle have the theology?

3. What are the four circle of theology?

4. What did God give the human through the doctrine?

5. What is the human identity?

6. What is to be?

7. What is to do?

About the Pastor

1. What is Pastor?

There is pastor whom God called according to His will.

Nu 16:7 - The man the Lord chooses will be the one who is holy.

De 21:5 - For the Lord your God has chosen them to minister and to pronounce blessings in the name of the Lord and to decide all cases of dispute and assault.

Isa 41:8 - You, O Israel, my servant, Jacob, whom I have chosen, you descendants of Abraham my friend.

Jn 15: 16 - You did not choose me, but I chose you and appointed you to go and bear fruit - fruit that will last. Then the Father will give you whatever you ask in my name.

Eph 1:4 - For he chose us in him before the creation of the world to be holy and blameless in his sight, In love.

If God calls someone as a pastor, He gave him His power and authority.

Mar 3:14~15 - He appointed twelve - designating them apostles- that they might be with him and that he might send them out to preach and to have authority to drive out demons.

Lk 22:35 - Jesus asked them, When I send you without purse, bag or sandals, did you lack anything? Nothing, they answered.

1. The pastor is person who commits God's will to the people.

Ex 39:43 - Moses inspected the work and saw that they had done it just as the Lord had commanded, So

De 18:18 - I will raise up for them a prophet like you from among their brothers; I will put my words in his mouth, and he will tell them everything I command him.

Je 1:7 - The Lord said to me, Do not say, I am only a child. You must go to everyone I send you to and say whatever I command you.

So Moses blessed them.

1Co 11:23 - For I received from the Lord what I also passed on to you.

Rev 22:18~9 - I warn everyone who hears the words of the prophecy, of this book: If anyone adds anything to them, God will add to him the plagues described in this book.

And if anyone takes words away from this book of prophecy, God will take away from him his share in the tree of life and in the holy city, which are described in this book.

When the human meet a even about something, we have to solve according to the God's will.

1. The Pastor's title is holy one of the best in the world.

Lu 1:70 - As he said through his holy prophets of long ago.

Eph 3:5 - Which was not made known to men in other generations as it has now been revealed by the Spirit to God's holy apostles and prophets.

1Pe 2:5 - You also, like living stones, are being built into a spiritual house to be a holy priesthood, offering spiritual sacrifices acceptable to God through Jesus Christ.

1. The Pastor is the forepart of sheep and they are not shepherd. The shepherd is only Christ Jesus.

Act 20:28 - Keep watch over yourselves and all the flock of which the Holy Spirit has made you overseers. Be shepherds of the church of God, which he bought with own blood.

1Ti 2:5 - For there is one God and one mediator between God and men, the man Christ Jesus.

Exercise

1. Who calls someone as pastor?

2. If God calls someone as pastor, what He gives him?

3. Who God's will commits to the people?

4. How do we do, when we meet something event?

5. What is the pastor's title?

6. Is the pastor shepherd?

About Pastor's ability

1. When God made the human, He gave them their ability to each one.

Ability of the human does not make themselves.

1Co 7:7 - I wish that all men were as I am, But each man has his own gift from God; one has this gift, another has that.

Ro 12:6 - We have different gift, according to the grace given us. If a man's gift is prophesying , let him use it in proportion to his faith.

Eph 4:11 - It was he who gave some to be apostles, some to be prophets some to be evangelists, and some to be pastors and teachers.

1. Ability is gift that one of best in the world is me myself.

We call it ability or talent.

There is different that God gives us to each one.

So when we work for church, there isn't way of us but true. God wants true of us.

1sa 16:7 - The Lord said to Samuel, Do not consider his

appearance or his height, for I have rejected him. The Lord does not look at the things man looks at. Man looks at the outward appearance, but the Lord looks at the heart.

Pr 4:23 - Above all else, guard your heart, for it is the wellspring of the life.

1. The Pastor's ability is like an apostle, prophet and king.

So the pastors aren't the apostle, prophet and king.

We really have to proud of characters.

1Ti 2:5 - For there is one God and one mediator between God and men, the man Christ Jesus.

1. The pastor's ability is the Evangelists and Teachers.

Mt 28:19~20 - Therefore go and make of all nations baptizing them in the name of the Father and of the Son and of the Holy Spirit, teaching them to obey them everything I have commanded you and surely I am with you and always to the end of the age.

Act 15:35 - Paul and Barnabas remained in Antioch, where they and many others taught and preached the word of the Lord.

1. The pastor's ability is perpetual ordinary.

So the pastor has to die for his church.

Act 26:12 - On one of these journeys I was going to Damascus with the authority and commission of the chief priests.

Nu 3:3 - Those were the names of Aaron's son's, the anointed priests, who were ordained to serve as priests.

1. The pastor's ability has to do worship, ceremony of sacrament and discipline.

Jn 4:24 - God is spirit His worshipers must worship in spirit and in truth.

1Co 11:23~25 - For I received from the Lord what I also passed on to you; The Lord Jesus, on the night he was betrayed, took bread, and when he had given thanks, he broke it and said, This in my body, which is for you do this in remembrance of me. In the same way, after supper he took the cup, saying, This cup is the new covenant in my blood; do this whenever you drink it, in remembrance of me.

2Ti 3:16 - All Scripture is God-breathed and is useful for teaching, rebuking, correcting and training in righteousness. so that the man of God may be thoroughly equipped for every good work.

Exercise

1. When God was the human, What God gave them?

2. What is gift that one of the best in the world?

3. What is that?
   There is (   ) that God gives us each one.

4. What is pastor's ability?
   Is it true or false?

5. The pastor's ability is Evangelists and Teachers.
   true (   ) false (   )

6. The pastor's ability is an ordinary of perpetual.
   true (   ) false (   )

7. The pastor's ability has to do worship, ceremony of sacraments
   and discipline.
   true (   ) false (   )

About the life of Pastor

1. The pastor has to live according to the word of God.

If we who are His children, have believed in Him, we have to such things.

It is that there are ten command in the old testament and the teaching mountain in the new testament.

What is purpose of Christianity?

We are that we are growing up like Christ Jesus.

1. We can laugh as we grew up our life.

We should do under sentence for character of us.

We always read the Bible.

We always pray to God.

We always attend to worship in the Lord days.

We usually should read piety books.

We should do under sentence for health of body.

We need to full of sleep.

We need to full of rest.

We need to full of exercise.

We need to eat proper foods.

1. We should live for the community of life.

We are the light and the salt of the world.

Mt 5:13~14 - You are the salt of the earth, But if the salt loses its saltiness, how can it be made salty again? It is no longer good for anything, except to be thrown out and trampled by men. You are the light of the world. A city on a hill cannot be hidden.

Mt 19:19 - Love you your neighbor as yourself.

The meaning of verses are that when you meet something event, you shouldn't escape from this one.

If we solve event something, we have to find God's meaning in it.

Because God rules nature cosmos and history of human.

1. Pastor has good manner to the neighbor.

1Ti 3:7 - He must also have a good reputation with outsiders, so that he will not fall into disgrace and into the devil's trap.

Tit 1:8 - Rather he must be hospitable, one who loves what is good, who is self-controlled, upright, holy and disciplined.

1. Pastor has habit of listening to the neighbor's voice.

Everything in the world is a voice of God. we should hear that.

Mt 6:26,30 - Look at the birds of the air; they do not sow or reap or store away in barns, and yet your heavenly father feeds them. Are you not much more valuable than they?

If that is how God clothes the grass of the field, which is here today and tomorrow is thrown into the fire, will he not much more clothe you, o you of little faith?

The Bible was written as point of savior. We should think that the way of nature cosmos and the way of history human as the Law of God.

1. Pastor has to be do the promise of each other.

Mt 20: 13~14 - He answered one of them, Friend, I am not being unfair to you. didn't you agree to work for a denarius? Take your pay and go. I want to give the man who was hired last the same as I gave you.

Heb 6: 13~15 - When God made his promise to Abraham, since there was no one greater for him to swear by, he swore by himself, saying, I will surely bless you and give you many descendants. And so after waiting patiently, Abraham received what was promised.

Exercise

1. If we have believed Him who are His children, how do we live?

2. What is purpose of Christianity?

3. What should we do for character of us?

4. What should we do for health of body?

5. If we meet an event something, what do we do?

6. What kind of voice we have?

7. What do we do about promised to each other?

1. The pastor might have full of Holy Spirit.

Who is the christianity full of Holy Spirit?

It is person who clearly lives according to the word of God.

The people who lives according to the word of God has appealed fruits to revelation of general.

The situations of revelation of general are love, holy, serve, free, dream, diligently and pure etc.

These have good keeping a point.

The church isn't growing up through themselves higher character.

If the christianity lives according to the word of God and lives to full of Holy Spirit, could growing up higher character.

Let us consider according to the Bible.

Phi 3:16 - Only what let us live up to what we have already attained.

Ge 13:9 - Is not the whole land before you? Let's part company. If you go to the left, I will go right. If you go the right; I will go to the left.

Mt 26:39 - Going a little farther, he fell with his face to the ground and prayed, My Father if it is possible may this cup be taken from me, Yet not as I will but as You will.

1. The pastor has to speak only God's word.

Jn 16:13~14 - When He the Spirit of truth comes, He will guide you into all truth. He will not speak in His own He will speak only what He hears. He will tell you what is yet to come He will bring glory to me by taking from what is mine and making it known to you.

Pastor is not a mediator between God and man, but only Christ Jesus be.

1 Ti 2:5 - For there is one God and one mediator between God and man, the man Christ Jesus.

Exercise

1. What does the pastor full to?

2. Who is full of Holy Spirit?

3. What kind of fruit does person who full of Holy Spirit appeal?

4. Is the church growing up through themselves higher character?

5. What is only pastor speak to?

6. Does the pastor become a mediator between God and man?

About worship

1. The worship is that christian confesses Christ Jesus through Holy Spirit.

Jn 4:24 - God is the Spirit the worshipers must worship with spirit and in truth.

1. The definition of worship, we find out three feasts and five offerings of Judea.

Three feasts are the Feast of passover, the Feast of week and the Feast of Tabernacle.

The five offerings are the burnt offering, cleaning offering, fellowship offering, sin offering and guilt offering.

1. The purpose of worship comes at the three Feasts of Judea.

First is the Feast of passover.

The Feast of passover that is to the memory of a cross of Jesus.

Eph 2:1 - We were died in our sins and transgression, but because the Christ Jesus was died a cross we were raised again.

Second is the Feast of week.

The Feast of week that is to the memory of the Ten commandments which Moses received from God in the Exodus chapter 20 and Deuteronomy chapter 5.

It is the words of God. So the words of God is the compass of life.

We can't live with our life on the world without compass of the words of God.

Third is the Feast of Tabernacle.

The Feast of Tabernacle is to the memory of thanksgiving day.

The meaning of Tabernacle is one among the God's temple.

The Temple's master is God.

The Temple's head is Christ Jesus.

1. The christianity is the body of Christ Jesus.

1Co 3:16 - Don't you know that you yourselves are God's temple and God's

Spirit lives in you.

That is right.

The Feast of Tabernacle is to the memory of thanksgiving day.

Because God goes with us of all our life.

1. The way of worship find out five offerings.

The five offerings are burnt offering, cleaning offering, fellowship offering, sin offering and guilt offering.

The burnt offering is to burn all on the alter.

The meaning is to the memory of death.

The cleaning offering is to the memory of pure. It looks to become like Christ Jesus.

When people offered cleaning offering, if people were poor, they offer sheep or dove or wheat instead of cow,

The fellowship offering is to the memory of between God and human, and among people.

The sin offering is to the memory of removing of sin to God.

The guilt offering is to the memory of removing sin before human being.

Exercise

1. What is definition of worship?

2. Where does the definition of worship come?

3. Where does the purpose of worship come?

4. What are the three feast of Judea?

5. Where does the way of worship come?

6. What are the fifth offering of Judea?

7. What is the meaning of burnt offering?

About the Education

1. The substance of Christianity education is the way of Holy Father, Holy Son and Holy Spirit.

God created the human as God's image.

Ge 1:17 - So God created man in His own image, in the image of God He created him; male and female He created them.

God had come as human on the earth by Himself to see to human. This was incarnation that the human could see Himself.

He works plan, providence, creation, rule, going, coming, standing, and handing over so on.

He appeared to us as Holy, love, peace, forever, judgment, don't change mind and freedom so on.

What is the substance of Holy?

God told us that Holy Himself is only ME, which God is the Holy. So we see God as the Holy.

If we asked what is Holy, no body can answer.

When we can see God, we can see really Holy, love, peace, and so on. Because God came incarnation on the earth.

Jn 1:14 - The word became flesh and made his dwelling among us, we have seen his glory and the glory the one and only who came from the Father's side, full of grace and truth.

Jn 14: 8~9 - Philip said Lord show us the Father and that will be enough for us Jesus answered Don't you know me, Philip even after I have been among you such a long time Anyone who has seen Me has seen the Father how can you say show us the Father?

1. The model of christian education is history of Judea.

They lived to be scattered on the world during about 2,000 years. But they lived as one nation. Because they learned their education.

Dt 6:4~9 - Hear O Israel; The Lord our God, the Lord is one. Lord the Lord your God with all your heart and with all your soul and with all your strength. These commandments that I give you today are to be upon your hearts. Impress them on your children. Talk about them when you sit at home and when you walk along the road, whin you lie down and when you get up. Tie them as symbols on your hands and bind them on your foreheads. Write them on the door frames of your houses and on your gates.

1. The model of Christian education is Christ Jesus.

It is that Christ Jesus was looked as model. the model crossed for us. So because Christ Jesus is model, we have to die like Christ jesus.

Phi 3:16 - only let us live up to what we have already attained.

Jn 13:13~15 - You call me Teacher and Lord and rightly so, for that is what I am. Now that I, your Lord and Teacher, have washed your feet, you also should wash one another's feet. I have set you an example that you should do as I have done for you.

Our teacher is Christ Jesus.

Mt 11:28~30 - Come to me, all you who ate weary and burdened, and I will give you rest. Take my yoke upon you and learn from me, for I am gentle and humble in heart, and you will find rest for your souls. For my yoke is easy and my burden is light.

Exercise

1. What is the substance of Christianity education?

2. What is the substance of Holy?

3. If we asked what is the substance of Holy to the human, what does human answer?

4. What is the model of Christianity education?

5. How many years is Israelite scattered to live abroad?

6. Who is model of Christianity education?

7. If the Christ Jesus is the model of Christianity education, how do we live?

About Mission

1. The mission is great commission as one's dying of Christ Jesus.

The starting mission isn't the human but God is.

God wants first important that the human calls Himself God.

If the human calls God, God gives His life to him.

God Himself is the missionary.

Jn 3:16 - God so loved world that He gave us His the one and only Son and that whoever believed Him shall not be perished but have eternal life.

Jn 20:21 - Again Jesus said peace be with you! As the Father has sent me, I am sending you.

Ro 5:8 - God demonstrate His own love for us in this; while we were still sinners, Christ died for us.

1. The mission is to obey according to the words of God.

Jn 15:12 - My command is this; Love each other as I have loved you.

Mt 28:19~20 - Go and make disciples of all nations baptizing them in the name of the Father and of the Son and of the Holy Spirit and teaching them obey them everything written in it then surely I am with you and to the very end of the age.

Act 1:8 - You will be received power when the Holy Spirit comes on you, you will be my witnesses in Jerusalem in all Judea and Samaria and to the end of the earth.

1. The mission is that the human doesn't call God but God has chosen and predestined the human.

Act 4:28 - They did what your power and will had decided beforehand should happen.

Eph 1:4~5 - For He chose us in Him before the creation of the world to be holy and blameless in his sight. in love He predestined us to be adopted as his sons through Jesus Christ, in accordance with his pleasure and will.

Isa 45:4 - For the sake of Jacob my servant, of Israel my chosen, I summon you by name and bestow on you a title of honor, though you do not acknowledge me.

We don't know person whom chose and predestined among the people. but we have to witnesses Him to the people.

1. The mission is roadway of blessing.

The Lord is always with them.

Mt 28:20 - Sure I am with him always to the very end of the age.

Lk 22:35 - Then Jesus asked them, When I sent you without

purse, bag or sandals, did you lack anything? Nothing, they answered.

Jn 8:29 - The one who sent me is with me; he has not left me alone, for I always do what pleases him.

Rev 3:20 - Here I am I stand at the door and knock if anyone hears my voice and open the door and I will come in and eat with him and he is with Me.

Exercise

1. What is the mission?

2. Who is starting mission?

3. What does missionary according to?

4. Does Missionary chose himself his mission work?

5. Who chose the missionary ?

6.What is the Lord's command?

7. What is the missionary's way?

About glorification

1. Glorification is order of God that we give glory to Him.

Isa 43:21 - The people I formed for myself that they may proclaim my praise.

Ps 100:1~3 - Shout for joy to the Lore, all the earth. Worship the Lord with gladness' come before him with joyful songs. Know that the Lord is God. It is he who made us, and we are his; we are his people, the sheep of his pasture.

So we should sing to praise according to order of God.

We should be know when we sing hymnal songs.

They have got two kinds of themselves.

One is worship song of God and the other is gospel song which we confess of our faith.

Worship songs were written about 1- 200 pages and gospel songs was written about 200-550 pages.

When we sing hymnal songs, we need balance of power to each other.

1. Who sings hymnal song?

We have to sing christianity. Because God orders us.

Isa 43:21 - The people I formed for myself that they may proclaim my praise.

Ps 150:1,6 - Praise the Lord. Praise God in his sanctuary; praise Him in His mighty heavens. Let everything that has breath praise the Lord. Praise the Lord.

1Co 10:31 - So whether you eat or drink or whatever you do, do it all for the glory of God.

1. Why do we sing hymnal song?

We have to sing that God came to us for saving us and that He is with us.

Isa 25:1 - O Lord, you are my God; I will exalt you and praise your name, for in perfect faithfulness you have done marvelous things, things planned long ago.

Isa 44:21 - Remember these things, for the Lord has done this; shout aloud, O earth beneath. Burst into song, you mountains, you forests and all your trees, for the Lord has redeemed Jacob, he displays his glory ins Israel

Heb 13:15 - Through Jesus, therefore, let us continually offer to God a sacrifice of praise - the fruit of lips that confess his name.

1. How do we sing hymnal song?

We should sing as our heart.

We should sing as our faith.

We should sing as our hands in high.

We should sing as our joyful life.

We should sing as our thanksgiving.

1Co 14:15 - So what shall I do? I will pray with my spirit, buy I will also pray with mind; I will sing with my spirit, but I will also with my mind.

Co 3:16 - Let the world of Christ dwell in your richly as you teach and admonish one another with all wisdom, and as you sing psalms, hymns and spiritual songs with gratitude in your heart to God.

Eph 5:19 - Speak to one another with psalms, hymns and spiritual songs. Sing and make music in your heart to the Lord.

Ps 100: 1~2 - Shout for joy to the Lord, all the earth.

Worship the Lord with gladness; come before him with joyful songs.

1. When do we sing hymnal song?

We should sing day by day with each passing moment, while we live in the world.

ps 1:2 - His delight is in the Law of the Lord, and on his Law he meditate day and night.

Ps 119:97 - Oh, how I love your law! I meditate on it all day long.

Isa 35:10 - The ransomed of the Lord will return. They will enter Zion with singing; everlasting joy will crown their heads. Gladness and joy will overtake them, and sorrow and sighing will flee away.

Exercise

1. What is the glorification?

2. What kind of way of sing, has the hymns book got?

3. What is two way of sing of hymns song?

4. Who sing hymns song?

5. Why sing hymns song?

6. How sing hymns song?

7. When sing hymns song?

About Administration

1. Administration treats an event. The human meets an event. The event has got a lot of things.

The event is like wind which are "give, take, eat, come, go, love, hate, gain and lose" etc.

The wind has got three special things.

The one is that the wind(event) is passing on.

The other is that the wind(event) is made through me.

Another is that the wind (event) is achieved through God's will.

Phi 3:16 - Only let us live up to what we have already attained.

Phi 4:6~7 - Do not be anxious about anything but in everything by prayer and petition with thanksgiving present your requesting your God Then the peace of God which transcends all understanding will guard in your heart and your mind in Christ Jesus.

1. The administration has been done in the center of God.

The master of Church is God because God made the Church.

Ex 25:8~9 - Then have them make a sanctuary for me, and I will dwell among them. Make this tabernacle and all its furnishings exactly like the pattern I will show you.

Mt16:18 - And I tell you that you are Peter, and on this rock I will build my church, and the gates of Hades will not overcome it.

Ps 132:13~14 - For the Lord has chosen Zion, he has desired it for his dwelling; This is my resting place for ever and ever; here I will sit enthroned, for I have desired it.

1. A point of connection between God and men is free (will).

The free is free of conscience and free of church.

Ge 2:16~17 - And the Lord God commanded the man, You are free to eat from amy tree in the garden; but you must not eat from the tree of the knowledge of good and evil, for when you eat of it you will surely die.

We know that we can eat the fruit or can't eat the fruit.

This is really free.

2 Co 9:6~7 - Remember this whoever sows sparingly will also reap harvest whoever sows generously will also reap harvest generously each of us should give what he has decided in his heart to give not reluctantly and under compulsion for God loves cheerful giver.

So it is very important that someone is not right through event but what God's will is.

1. The way of pastoral ministry has got uncountable a lot.

It is not the way a pastoral but it is important people who are honest and eagerness in their heart

1 Sa 16:7 - But the Lord said to Samuel, Do not consider his appearance or his height, for I have rejected him. The Lord does not look at the things man looks at. Man looks at the outward appearance, but the Lord looks at the heart.

Pr 4:23 - Above all else guard your heart for it is the wellspring of life.

1. The political of church belong to gospel of God.

The gospel said that the christian died for neighbor.

Mk 10: 45 - For even the son of man did not come to be served but to serve and to give His life as a ransom for many.

Jn 13:14 - Now that I, your Lord and Teacher, have washed your feet, you also should wash one another's feet.

1. The political of church is being with church.

Jn 3:16 - God so loved world that He gave us His one and only son that whoever believes in Him and shall not perish but have eternal life.

1Co 9:19 - Though I am free and belong to no men I myself make a slave to everyone and to win as many as possible.

1. The political of church responses to the public.

Mt 5:13~14 - You are the salt of the earth. But if the salt loses its saltiness, how can it be made saltly again? It is no longer good for anything, except to be thrown out and trampled by men.

You are the light of the world. A city on a hill cannot be hidden.

Ro 16:25~27 - Now to him who is able to establish you by my gospel and the proclamation of Jesus Christ, according to the revelation of the mystery hidden of long ages psst, but now revealed and made known through the prophetic writings by the command of the eternal god, so that all nations might believe and obey him to the only wise God be glory forever through Jesus Christ! Amen.

Exercise

1. What does the administration treat?

2. The event namely wind has got three special.
   What are these?

3. What is the point of connect between God and men?

4. What is important people?

5. Who does the political of church belong to?

6. Which is the political of church being with?

7. Which does the political of church response?

About desires

1. What is desire?

The desire is to be namely nature of human according to Korean dictionary.

It is nature which God gives human.

However Bible said Ro 3:23 - All have sinned and fall short of the glory of God.

Isa 53:6 - We have like sheep have gone astray each of us has turned his own way the Lord has laid on Him iniquity for us all.

We must give attention to this.

Because we have sinned, we have gone astray, and we have turned to our own way.

So we have fallen short of the glory of God.

We should think about that.

Do we leave God or does desire leave God?

Yes. We left God and the desire was being as nature.

At this point,

I and desire are different.

I leave God.

You leave God.

He and She leave God.

I, You and He or She are one of them.

We all are the singular.

It become known to us that desire itself can leave or can't leave.

Ge 2:15~16 - The Lord God commanded the man you are free to eat any fruit in the garden but you must not eat from at tree of the knowledge of good and evil for when you eat of it you will be surely die.

Here,

They could be eat and couldn't be eat.

Their desires are really free yet.

We know that they ate forbidden fruit and they surely died.

They died surely because they ate them.

That is right.

Our desires and their desires are the same.

If so,

How do we use our desires?

It is very important.

Now we are also free.

Therefore how do we use our desires?

We have to use our desires for the glory of God.

I explain in another way.

Jesus said to us through Bible.

Lk 9:23 - If anyone would come after me he must deny himself and take up his cross daily and follow me.

I think that I also mean the same as that.

My death is what I must deny myself.

Here,

"My death" and "I must deny myself" are different.

What are they different?

My death is "me" and my desire is that I must deny myself.

I said that desire is to be namely nature that comes from ourselves. We can't kill them.

If that so,

What does "kill desire" mean?

This mean is to use desire to the standard of God.

When we use to be natural, we must use to do to the standard of God. and we can't use desire without the standard of God.

I'm worried how should I use my desire?

I'd like to use them for the glory of God. I don't hate desire but I want to use desire well. Because God gives us the desire.

I dislike them but I must only use well.

I say lastly. 1Co 10:31- So whether you eat or drink or whatever you do, do it all for the glory of God.

Answer of Exercise

About Pastoral theology

1. It is a medical center.

2. They are the people who are called according to God's will.

3. They know that the pastors are using the Biblical theology, dogmatics theology and practical theology.

4. It is only God.

5. It is the sovereign power of God.

6. No it isn't .

7. It is the one.

8. It is the death.

9. One is to obey of the Law of God.

   the other is completion of the Law of God.

About always present

1. It is a present.

2. Because the human left God.

3. They live with past, present and feature.

4. It is God's order.

5. We always eat an event.

6. This is the Law of God which made God.

7. He is with us to the very end of the age.

About Pastoral

1. It is the pastoral.

2. It looks like Christ Jesus.

3. It looks like Christ Jesus.

4, It is Christ Jesus.

5. It is the word of God.

6. It takes make a rest.

7. It is Holy Spirit.

About the foundation of pastoral

1. It is the Bible.

2. It is the Bible.

3. We can find out two circles.

4. One is Christ Jesus.

   the other is Immanuel.

5. Christ Jesus is savior, messias so on.

6. Immanuel is that God is with us.

About Historical foundation

1. It is the Theology.

2. They have four circles.

3. They are Bible theology, Dogmatics theology, Historical theology and Practical theology.

4. He gave us Human identity.

5. It is about that there are to be and to do.

6. They are God, Human(home), the church(nation), the word of God (Bible) and the History(Nature).

7. They are

    * The Law of Holy Father, Holy Son and Holy Spirit.

    * The Law of worship, faith and pray.

    * The Law is that the human is analysis and God is conclusion.

    * The Law is that there are only different explaining but really the meaning is the one.

    * The Law is that the reward is in accordance with a deeds.

    * The Law is that they all are saying Yes.

About Pastor

1. It is God according to His will.

2, It is power and authority.

3. It is God.

4. We have to solve according to the God's will.

5. It is the Holy one of the best in the world.

6. No it is not.

About Pastor's ability

1. He gave them their ability to each other.

2. It is me myself.

3. It is different.

4. It is like an apostle, prophet and king.

5. It is true.

6. It is true.

7. It is true.

About like of pastor

1. It is that there are ten command of old testament and the teaching mountain of new testament.

2. It is that we are growing up like Christ Jesus.

3. We always read the Bible, pray to God, attend to worship of the Lord day.

4. We need to full of sleep, of rest, of exercise and to eat reasonable food.

5. We shouldn't escape from this one.
   We have to find God's mean in it.

6. It has a habit of listening about neighbor voice.

7. We have to be done.

About the goal of pastor

1. It is the Holy Spirit.

2. It is person who lives according to the word of God.

3. It is appealed fruit to revelation of general.

4. No it isn't.

5. He has to speak only God's word.

6. No it does not become a mediator between God and men.

About worship

1. It is that the Christianity confess Christ Jesus through Holy Spirit.

2. It comes three feast and fifth offering or Judea.

3. It comes three feast of Judea.

4. There are the Feast of passover, week and Tabernacle.

5. It comes fifth offering of Judea.

6. There are burnt offering, cleaning offering, fellowship offering, sin offering and guilt offering.

7. The meaning is memory which is death.

About education

1. It is way of Holy Father , Holy Son and Holy Spirit.

2. It is Himself God.

3. They couldn't answer about it.

4. It is the history of Judea.

5. It is about 2000 years.

6. It is a Christ Jesus.

7. We have to die for neighbor, because Christ Jesus cross for our sins.

About mission

1. It is great commission as one's dying of Christ Jesus.

2. It is God.

3. It is according to the word of God.

4. No He and She couldn't chose this one.

5. It is God.

6. As I have loved you love each other.

7. It is blessing.

About glorification

1. We sing that we give the glory to God.

2. It has got two kind of hymns on the Book.

3. One is worship song and the other is gospel song.

4. We have to sing us.

5. We have to sing that God comes to me to save us and He is with me.

6. We should sing as heart, faith, our joyful, give thanks and life my hands in high.

7. We should sing day by day with each passing moment, while I live in the world.

About administration

1. It is an event.

2. The one is that event is passing on.

   The other is that through event is made become me.

   One other is that through event achieve God's will.

3. It is the free.

4. It is honest and eagerness in their heart.

5. It is the gospel of God.

6. It is the church.

7. It is the public.

The definition of resurrection
1Co 15 : 3-4

There is the words the human can't speak but only God can.

This is that It is finished.

I am who I am.

Your sins are forgiven.

I am the way and the true and the life.

I will set you free.

I am the Alpha and the omega.

The resurrection also is the same thing.

We can heard the voice of resurrection through the Scripture.

Let us consider through the it.

*The resurrection is the act of historical.

Ac 1:11

Men of Galilee, they said, why do you stand here looking into the sky? This same Jesus, who has been taken from you into heaven, will come back in the same way you have seen him go into heaven.

*The resurrection is conclusion and flower of christianity.

1Co 15:20-22

Christ has been raised from the dead, the first fruits of those who have fallen asleep. for since death came through a man, the resurrection of the dead comes also through a men. for as in Adam all die, so in Christ all will be made alive.

*If resurrection is noting, the christianity will be end religion of ethics.

Gal 4:3-6

So also, when we were children, we were in slavery under the basic principles of the world. But when the time had fully God sent his Son, born of a women, born under law. to redeem those under law that we might receive the full rights of sons. Because you are sons, God sent the Spirit of his Son into our hearts, the Spirit who calls out, Abba, Father.

*If Christ has not been raised, your faith is futile and we are   to be pitied more than all men

1 Co 15:16-19

For if the dead are not raised, then Christ has not been raised either. and if Christ has not been raised, your faith is futile; you are still in your sins. The those also who have fallen asleep in Christ are lost. If only for this life we have hope in Christ, we are to be pitied more than all men.

*The resurrection is the first fruit of those who have fallen asleep.

1 Co 15: 20-22

But Christ has indeed been raised from the dead, the first fruits of those who have fallen asleep. For since death came through a man, the resurrection of the dead comes also through a man. For as in Adam all die, so in Christ all will be made alive.

*The resurrection fixed point of solve of event of our life.

Ro 8:37-39

No, in all these things we are more than conquerors through him who loved us. For I am convinced that neither death nor life, neither angels nor demons, neither the present nor the future, nor any powers, neither height nor depth, nor anything else in all creation, will be able to separate us from the love of God that is in Christ Jesus our Lord.

*The resurrection is substance of perfection of our life.

1Co 15: 55-58

Where, O death, is your victory? Where, O death, is your sting? The sting of death is sin, and the power of sin is the law. But thanks be to God! He gives us the victory through our Lord Jesus Christ. Therefore, my dear brothers, stand firm. let nothing move you. Always give yourselves fully to the work of the Lord, because you know that your labor is not in vain.

*The resurrection is that our christian is glory of God and we are really sanctuary for your dwelling.

Ex 15: 17-18

The place oh Lord you made for your dwelling, the Lord sanctuary your hand's established, Oh Lord will reign for ever and ever.

*The resurrection is living hope of our life.

Jn 11: 25-26

Jesus said to her I am the resurrection and the life. He who believes in me will live, even though he dies; and whoever lives and believes in me will never die. Do you believe this?

*The resurrection gives us perfect peace of our life.

Isa 26:3

You will perfect peace him whose mind steadfast is mind, because he trusts in You.

*The resurrection gives us really rest.

Mt 11: 28-30

Come to me, all you who are weary and burdened, and I will give you rest. Take my yoke upon you and learn from me, for I am gentle and humble in heart, and you will find rest for your souls. For my yoke is easy and my burden is light.

*The resurrection is filling up the desire of human character.

Heb 2:18

Because He Himself suffered when He was tempted, He is able to help those who are being tempted.

*The resurrection is answer one of best in the world about where the human goes to and come from.

Ro 11:36

For from him and through him and to him are all things.

*The resurrection gives us freedom from all of things.

It is from the desires.

It is from the satan.

It is from the commandments>

It is from the cause and effect.

1 Co 9:19

Though I am free belong to no man I myself make slave to everyone to win as many as possible.

Gal 5:13

You my brothers, were called to be free do not use your freedom to indulge the sinful nature; rather serve one another in love.

*The resurrection is made living to see the truth while we live in the world.

Because of the resurrection, the truth only be appealed as truth.

Jn 12:45

When he looks at me, he sees the one who sent me.

1Co 15:51-52

Listen, I tell you a mystery: We will not all sleep, but we will all be changed- in a flash, in he twinkling of an eye at the last trumpet. For the trumpet will sound, the dead will be raised imperishable, and we will be changed.

*The resurrection gives us be being live forever as long as we live.

Jn 6:35

Then Jesus declared, I am the bread of life, he who comes to me will never go hungry, and he who believes in me will never be thirsty.

Rev 22:13

I am the Alpha and the Omega, the First and the Last, the Beginning and the End.

Lovely children of God!

Do you believe resurrection of Christ Jesus? We have to trust it.

The Holy Spirit comes among us we have to been made believed Christ Jesus. This is promise of God for us.

We have to been seen as model of our life for our neighbor.

We are always the life of resurrection as day by day and with each passing moment.